T0386144

Heather Sellers

The Boys I Borrow

New Issues Poetry & Prose

A Green Rose Book

New Issues Poetry & Prose
The College of Arts and Sciences
Western Michigan University
Kalamazoo, Michigan 49008

An Inland Seas Poetry Book

 Inland Seas poetry books are supported by a grant from
The Michigan Council for Arts and Cultural Affairs.

First Edition, 2007.

ISBN-10   1-930974-71-X (paperbound)
ISBN-13   978-1-930974-71-5 (paperbound)

Library of Congress Cataloging-in-Publication Data:
Sellers, Heather
The Boys I Borrow/Heather Sellers
Library of Congress Control Number: 2007924970

Managing Editor   Marianne Swierenga
Copy Editor   Elizabeth Marzoni
Designer   Sherri Mealey
Art Director   Tricia Hennessy
Production Manager   Paul Sizer
                         The Design Center, School of Art
                         College of Fine Arts
                         Western Michigan University

The Boys I Borrow

Heather Sellers

New Issues

WESTERN MICHIGAN UNIVERSITY

Also by Heather Sellers

Poetry:

> *Your Whole Life* (chapbook)
> *Drinking Girls and Their Dresses*

Fiction:

> *Georgia Under Water*

Children's Literature:

> *Spike and Cubby's Ice Cream Island Adventure!*

On Writing:

> *Page After Page: How to Start Writing and Keep Writing No
> Matter What*
> *Chapter After Chapter: Discover the Dedication and Focus You
> Need to Write the Book of Your Dreams*
> *The Practice of Creative Writing*

for DWD, always

Contents

I.

SAT Words with David Jr. in His Father's Bed

We are on his dad's bed
On the comforter
Which is inimical
To our comfort and
David Jr. is pusillanimous.
And irascible. And petulant.
"These are all you," I say.
He says, "Stop talking, stop
Trying to help." He's afraid
Of these words, rightly so.
They scare their recipients.
Hard to pronounce, these words
Snootify and do not truly
Amplify the meanings they
Promise. "I already know,"
He says, "Give me 'stipend.'
Stop shuffling the pack."
"Hazard," I say. "Maul, copious."
I call out the words looking
For an order that makes sense,
At least foretells, or just pleases
Me. He says, "This is not how I learn.
Stop giving me clues.
Stop moving the flashcards.
Stop talking. Stop using
Words in sentences.
That is not how I remember.
Stop saying 'good job!'
After every single word.
Cease." He says, "Heather.
You have a hole in your shirt."
The definition of which is
You are drinking wine.
You are not helping me.
You are Dad's girlfriend
I was listening outside the door
Last night and for some
Of the things that happen

In this house, there are not words.
But you pretend it can all be said.

The Language of the Couple

The tiniest anything in the sweet whole world
Is named new, just you two know bike is Pony,
Boy is Rug, van is Pookatron, husband, The Pook.
An adorable adoring dictionary feeds you two.
You have your names for each other engraved
In your wedding rings, you have names for a chair,
The bed, the way you lean back when he holds you.
You name the compost pile, you name the dogs
Over and over and over with new and ever sicklier
Goopier names. Oh Bowser, oh Cutie. Oh Pookadoo.

No more named things the sons protest, it's just
Jake, stop, stop with The Bug, the June, Junie June Bug
Everything doesn't have to be
Named. They repeat.
Whatever.
The Less Said
The Better.

But it does. Everything does have to be named.
Naming's the knitting love does to keep you
Snug; it's the country you make,
The place you live in. Its language is a two-people
Fluency. The extra names gild a thing, a boy, a heart—
The more names the more loved. The more
Loved the more worth, the more you want it.

And so we continue
To summon the bicycle, the car, the garbage
Can, the boys, the hounds, the dishes, the heart
By the love names, the wings Words have when they are
Just yours and his, tongue of two of one of you.

Play House

The dad is David, roofer at nineteen. He has a son, rule slim.
Same name, same nose, same thorax and tones. Same broom handle bones.
After work (lug buckets of hot) & day care (everything is spilled) the Davids
Hole up with cereal in serving bowls in the back bedroom.

By the time I pull up, late, too fast, at an angle, into their lives, the
Two Davids are standing on the porch, which tilts. Tall skinny Dutch
American boys, still talking, still facing forward. Arms hang down like plumb
Lines. Hands fiddling with a clip and a clamp.

The cheap white vinyl porch door behind them, askew, a frame
Around version confusion. I look from one to the other.
Time slaps back and forth. "Hey, your dad said your stove has never
been plugged in?" I say. I admit I'm bounding up the porch stairs, I confess the

Wood feels pretend. Boys grin, men part. I'm in.
And overcome with the urge to boil water, bake cake, make stew, sweep.
Break down. I open the cupboards. One by one.
And the boys are laughing, edgy from everything that is not there.

After Meeting Your Mother

The mother of three girls, three boys,
Six, on Saturday afternoon in July,
I'm beside you, on her possessive
Bicycle, the Saratoga, its basket
Stuffed with my jacket, sunglasses, black
Hair clip. We are cutting through
The sand by Lake Michigan, a shocked
Open mouth on the baby face of the universe.
I'm talking too much and I'm holding
You back, you on your rotten boyhood
Racer. Because I'm uneasy.
Because I'm unsteady in the quivery
Sand. Because I accidentally met
Her in the upstairs hallway
When I went to pee.
She was in only a purple towel
Her long grey hair dripping
Wet on the old crazy hardwood.
We shook hands; she extended. I saw
A vein on her thigh, violet as her eyes.
I saw an antique crib in a bedroom. I tried
Not to look at any of this, kept my eyes open
But I looked up.

Once in awhile I get pregnant but
Each time I seem to pay
Too close attention; my body
Doesn't ever forget anything,
Not for one solitary second.
I can't coast or slide or not know.
Not one breath or beat can
Just be. Attention becomes
A form of attack; I lose each time.

From your Beachcomber bike
You reach in, flick my bell.
We never lock sprockets

Under the kites for sale
Along the beach path where
Two grade school boys wave
From the bed of a red pick up
Truck; we wave back, Hello hello!
As though we are successful
As though we are twins
As though we are the wind.

That night just before midnight,
Reading her books in our guest
Beds I remember seeing my hair
Clip fallen in the sand on Beach Street
A shiny black claw stuck in the red
Flowers—a sand-worthy kind—
They'll grow anywhere. Ones
She planted, with her club.

His Boys in My House

Say, let us rent books from
The library and drive your car. Let us explode
And buy gum and become.

We run through the living
Room with javelins. Little can be done.

Let us, unbathed, stab your hounds. Let us punch
And fart, snot, reject underwear.
Let us go commando and ogre and battle.

Let us bleed. We are the boys, we
Are the boys of your boyfriend.

And we find you enchanting. Like Leia.
Like Zelda, like her you are our not-mother,
You are pretty brown-haired Cindy in the blue dress

From Nintendo Harvest Moon. We love Cindy and
Bring her horses and crops. We love you, you who could date
Harry Potter, or be his dead glowing mom.

    *

And there was the night you saved us. Dad conked out.
You, checking on us, covering us with the quilt,
Ducked. There was a presence that night, a swooping

(In addition to adolescence.) You saw it and knew from its
Jagged crazy flight: The vampire bat! In our bedroom, your guest
Room swirling around our heads. We didn't know.

Until you screamed in your white gown, with lace, and ties
At the throat. We said Let us at him. We said let us play a little
Tennis with that bat! Let us examine these droppings on your white

Carpet, collect the whole bat business, take it to school.
Why not? That night, you floated us downstairs to safety,
Snugged us on the good sofa. On your sofa, bat-free and

Foot to head (the gown not so see through) we were warm and still.
Not unlike the living dead, whom we adore and hope to become. We felt:
Married. In love. It's good to be awake at three in the morning. With a girl.

                    *

God we hate jazz. Jazz is like long answers
To simple easy questions. What's afterlife? What
Is exactly a zombie? How do you pronounce B-O-S-O-M?

That last one, the bosom question we didn't mean to ask.
It was an accident.
We had no idea. None.

Your singing Eminem—it's you, trying to be like us, please don't.
Act your age. And Don't Ask. We do not know what happened
In school today, it's hours ago, we are not even sure

What's happening right now, and we will not remember.
We will remember your pink flimsy dress with the dots, and

Your favorite little rooster plate and that it was from your mother.
We were sad when you dropped it, it broke to smithereens. We enjoy
    smithereens.
Not hugging, exactly. Hugging is mysterious to us; we are wings and bones,
    never still.

This is because the pronunciation
Of the word bosom has been frightening our tongues ever since that day.
And we are sorry we asked the definition of That Word though it is worth
    remembering.

(Please note you did give as a present to us the book containing the word.)

We love it when we catch you kissing Dad even though we scream and
Cover our eyes. This is us acting normal. And we love your questions and
    we love
Our long no-eyed silences. We like the idea of hot cocoa, please don't be

Bothered that we do not actually drink it. Once it burned our tongues.
And it's in our tongues where we hold the memory of our mother,

In her kitchen, in a way only we taste her. It's a lot to put something in
    your body.

Our boy tongues are simple antennae.
We can't control them. Lick, lick, lap lap.
See we are dogs now. Hounds. Rabid.

Unchained, spilling only because we are wild uncontrollable hounds.

Okay. That was sloppy, sorry. Please forgive us and keep the cocoa
Coming. It's our ritual. We sit love to sit with the undrunk
At your Pottery Barn table, perfect for draping ourselves onto.

This is a good table. Butcher block? It doesn't seem to mind
Being kicked, nicked, or spilled upon and that is as it should be
For a table. We love knives. We would let you carve us into small pieces.

*

We have dreams of you and you are never naked.
You are never naked in these dreams. You are never naked.
Oh person in love with our father. Do you love him enough?

We do not wonder. Give us chores. We want you.
If only you didn't intervene. If only you played Slug Bug No Slug
Back in all fifty states, if you only enjoyed Risk as much as you
    said you would.

What a perfect boy you'd be, what a fellow, what a thing, what a nation-
    builder,
What a fighter, what a destroyer you could be, mother what a boy.

Ontology of Nintendo

And it's complicated because it's not. Down B.
Up C. The moves don't come naturally to my thumbs.
I manage my acre: a farm, crops, a stack of lumber.

Jake says "Get things to sell at Moon Mountain. Up C."
The game makes you automatically sleep. Skip
To the next day. Give the turnip to the Mayor's

Wife for a recipe. You get to name your dog.
How do you know all this? I ask Jacob. He has
Beaten the game. Many, many times. That's how.

To win, get married. You are trying to get married.
Meanwhile, upgrade sickle. Save money. Mash A.
Go to the field. You will have a scene. Take the pony.

Jacob says, "Yeah, you are good." He has to find Ellie.
He gives me tips: There's money under those rocks.
He says, "Here, let me be your guy for awhile."

It will be faster for me this way. Watch how he does it.
No one can stay single. Make sure you have fodder. For
The girls, for the horse your object: maintain happy.

"It's a nice change of pace to raise a farm," Jacob says.
"Normally I'm killing Zombies and saving the world.
That's pretty much all you need to know about me and my brother."

However there is always a secret level. Another season after winter;
You have a chance to be King. These are the last days. Go to any
Of the girls and propose. Jake wins me a Turtle Figurine. It matters.

I'm already at a secret level. This season, with boys and crops:
Apple juice, twin beds, the Dad. I want to live in this town that
Ends in a clear abyss of blue screen. This life where it's so clear

What can happen next, when you plant Moon Drop Seeds.
I say, "Jacob, when are you going to get married? For real."
"Married," he says. "Don't even say that. I have my whole life

Ahead of me." And Ann lights up. He has made her glowing.
"Ah," he says. "Heather, that's pretty much it." He gives me

The controls, "Now. You want to feed your dog. Any edible item. I'll stay. Until you are done."

Dating Men With Children

I'm the girlfriend.
The dad works

Late. Jake is the kid and
We play

Nintendo.
He is talking to priests

In peril all over the world,
He's at melee level.

It's very a difficult level
(We know from experience).

I wish my life
Was more like this:

Little dialog boxes,
Strange figures in Mauritania

In monk's robes, giving
Me light. My friend

Liz is is getting a divorce.
They have three

Kids. She said:
His lips burned.

Every time.
They kissed.

I'm scratching my lips.
Clicking Up C. No, Jacob says.

You just gave away
Your cloaking power.

I love the dad, but maybe
It's killing me. I like the kid.

Levelling up to Family.
Power me to the castle.

You want out of that room,
Jake says. Laser now.

There are dragons here.
(There were dragons there, too.)

Step Sons

I've got the boys

On my floor, brushed, shiny, under
A down comforter from my mother,

Cocoa on trays on their knees, a war
Documentary on screen

And you walk in and say, "They've
Never had it so good, baby. Boys,

How about this." You stand
In the doorway like a door. Not a key.

I'm surprised. I didn't know you
Thought this way. The boys turn their

Heads but not their eyes. Dirt
Explodes, and men. It's all going to spill.

Once, I took pleasure in confusing "father"
With words from other languages.

Now, I will keep the boys
Like this: covered.

It just needs to be simple. Mine.
You say this. What walls say.

I Get My Sons

Their chins betray me; I'm married only
A few weeks when my babies
Sprout black hairs, fierce little beard beginnings,
David Jr.'s darkening upper lip, Jake's chin
Hairing, tiny silver-black swords.
Hair, the body's
Coarse language, pokes its words at me:
Stay back.
We will spike you.
I'm helping them multiply fractions.
I can't remember if one reduces or cross multiplies
In this situation. I might not have ever
Known.

I want to have washed with
My thumbs and lavender
Their baby necks, bellies,
Bitten them and brushed their
Tongues and silk. Babies,
Edible and forever-lasting.
I'm nice. I'm not their mother.
They call Dad; he says Your x's are
Your unknowns, keep them on the same side.
ABCs are your knowns. Keep them
On the other side. I tell the boys:
This is a huge breakthrough.

I dream of holding
These huge boys
Long as canoes
Rocking them to sleep,
Whispering them back.
I dream of making them.

These not-sons, these semi-men,
They lurk in my house
Like their beardlings.
They strew their notebooks and shoes;

I needle and worry them, I pull.
Hey, how's it going?

They never ripped me,
Never took a quick
Bite. I get them as they're leaving.
I know them from the back.
Are you hungry? Do you want more?
My body isn't in the equation
And the math—not easy—is too clean.

You Suck

For soccer I drag Jake from his bed,
His window unit air conditioner,
His summer, his bowl of warm milk,
His monks in robes with runes. He tells me,

When I ask him to pull up the blue
Cans at the end of the driveway, the recycling bins
Emptied of their excess, so we can get out, now,
We have to go: Heather, you suck. And I do.

I do suck. Why do I ask him to do this chore?
Why does he do it, kicking cans up the drive,
Leaving them tipped on their sides? I could
Have done it. Why does he need "his job"?

Boys aren't born with sperm. After vasectomy
Most men make antibodies to attack sperm cells,
Unrecognizable invaders; what one isn't born with
Is automatically the enemy. Wombs are open bowls.

Round is the strongest shape on earth. This, the sorry
Truth. When he walks in the house, shouldering
Humiliation like a grey cloak, I followed, possible,
Complete, from day one, knowing, ruling.

Found Poem: Jacob's Homework Handout:
"Your Teen Pregnancy Statistics"

True.

A full quarter of teenage girls who are sexually active report
they are depressed all, most, or a lot of the time. Emotional
consequences. HIV. Serious infections. Cancers develop.
Death is the result.

Children of teen parents are more likely to
   __ have low birth weight
   __ be poor
   __ be incarcerated (put in jail).

Seven of ten fathers _____ the teen mother of their baby.
Teen fathers _____ than their peers.
Teens with older male sex partners are _____

What are some complications? Eye problems for infants.
Serious damage to pelvic organs.

Children of teen parents are less likely to
   __ graduate
   __ earn high income

Pubic lice can be cured by medicated soaps.

And . . . did you know . . . girls who were depressed in adolescence
were more than twice as likely to be obese in adulthood (at age 26).

Not to mention!

   __ broken heart
   __ feelings of insecurity
   __ loss of respect and self-respect
   __ feelings of guilt
   __ fear and worry
   __ feelings of being used
   __ tarnished reputation
   __ memories and comparisons

When Does Life Begin?

I think I know but the body doesn't
Have any sense. I found one baby
Not in my uterus, but nearby.

These things happen all the time. I am
Not an experiment, not a freak. It's nature,
The doctor says. He finally gives

Me baby-shrinking shots. There is no
Turning back. Once my doctor was forced by Michigan
Law to deliver a baby without a head.

We are going to have this not-baby
In little tiny pieces. This happens
All the time. Life is a mess. This baby

My last shot, my super-shot baby does
Not shrink. When does life begin?
It doesn't begin. Life roams without direction.

The shots make me lightning mad, electric
Tempered; everything grows fast, my hair
Ropes down my back. Operation Bad Seed.

Where does life end? Hospital paperwork
Titles this The Products of Conception.
The legislators are dead right: this is life.

There is weakness. There is distraction.
There is statistical frequency. There are
Counts. Sometimes when I fall, this is why.

Grocery Store Parking Lot, Winter in Michigan, No Children

I make my way across the lot
With a cart. Fennel, beans, paper, wine.
Seagulls slit the felt sky low
Over the parked cars. I know seagulls.

On a hill of black parking lot snow
Two boys throw down coats—their coats
Now dead bodies. And I am glad to see
The boys war on because of this carnage.

Daughters: wiggling under down
Comforters and wishing
Everything grey away, dolls
Forgiven again and again, girls whispering:

Go back down where you came from.
Sons: thirsty for ice, swords, stones.
One lung fire one lung
Ice. Like a zombie's.

My plastic sacks crinkling. My
House is filling up with plastic bags.
My eggs are spotted. I'm losing in months.
Open the wine.

Fennel seems poisonous on the counter.
I am pining for a close call. I go back
To the store before I really need anything.
It's fine if you are asking because

You want to know.

Grand Rapids Fertility Doctor's Office

There's too much empty space.
In the waiting room, no patients.
No receptionist, no assistant.
No windows, no clocks.
No magazines. No doorknobs.
No music. Five corn plants, green
Dull and wet, in fluorescence, fertility.
Swing doors. Bulletin board
Wide as the side of a bus.
Studded with baby Polaroids
Like porn. Maybe it's all the same baby.

Who is this doctor my husband's
Insurance provides, his desk
Empty? Who takes a phone
Call. "My daughter," he says
To us. The call takes a long time.
Evening is discussed, a cake, a mother.
Advice is given, repeated. He tells
Us she is expecting. He takes
Off his glasses and says
We have to really, really want
Children. He says it is not
Going to be what we think.
Most people would not if
They knew. As he talks, he taps
Silky black slides of the inside
Of my heart of hearts. The uterus
Is the only thing
Made of the same
Fiber as the heart. The cells
Are the same kind, same mission
In life. The lower heart. Older.
Maybe wiser. I'm dying for him to open

The folder, tell us. How many
Procedures, what operations, how much money.
"So," I say, impatient. My husband
Puts his arm around my shoulders, too

Heavy. The doctor taps his phone.
Willing it to ring? He flips the folder
With my husband's statistics. See? Bad.
We can't make heads or tails of
My husband's heads and tails. "Not good,"
Doctor says. "I do not judge who should
And should not have a baby."
There are no books in his
Office. I want to fling myself
Through the cement wall. I do
Judge: This can't be the point.
I married Dave, I married a father.
He says, "This isn't life or death,"
And I stand up to go. "There's worse,"
He says. I sit back down. I place
My hands on my husband's thigh,
His heartbeat there. In my head
I'm writing letters to commissions,
He's a nut, he can't place his hands
Inside of women, he can't access
Instruments and stainless theories.

"You, my dear, have a tumor," he says.
His phone rings. "Five tumors, one on
The fundus." He picks up the phone.
"The what?" I say. A mother would know.
"Where the baby attaches. It's the most
Important spot." I told you this would
Happen, he says into his phone.
He mouths to us, "Getting rid of tumors
Is a kind of birth itself." His hand
Over the talking part of the phone
Draped like a sheet. Back in my own
Lap, my fists. Eggs in a basket.
There's the end of most of it.
I've come here in my own car.

Hard Tail

You wish not to break up but slowly drift
Apart. No fissure no fracture. Nothing

Parting. I miss swimming in sinkholes,
Poems in Spanish, places

I made so that nothing would fall out of me.
Thanks, Mom! See you, Dad!

I'm trying to make you
My whole life. A middle aged woman

On a motorcycle trying to catch up to the girl
I was becoming; he hits the gas.

I can feel the shift.

Anniversary

Saturday night the boys kick us out
Of the house. "Come back.
We'll say when." I enter
The living room first through new
Purple curtains of tissue
Paper and I'm teary already.
Jake: "He even got the pitcher."
David holds the gravy boat
Aloft "What is this? What is this?"
And his dad says, "Oh
Buddy. You spent all
Your money." I see for weeks, he's
Socked away the weekly D&W
Featured dish, count nineteen plates,
Fourteen salad bowls, seven
Soup bowls, twenty cups and
Saucers plus the platter, the boat,
Six salt and peppers. "He went
Overboard," Jake says. "I did sign
The card. I knew you'd cry."
He shakes his head at his rightness.
And steps back from the dining
Room table, folding his arms
While David rearranges teacups
And grins and worries.

White dishes, with blue flowers.
A silver rim, leaves improbably pink
Sometimes the stamping is off a hair.
They've set the table, stacking
The dishes at our four places,
Each place a tower stack of dishes.
One place has five plates stacked,
Another has six. The bowls teeter like
Hats, up, up, up. No heads.
"It's your wedding china, basically,"
Jacob says, nodding approval.

The dishes stay on the table all
Week; we eat in the kitchen—
Pizza, standing, boxes, cans and
Pans and spoons. It hurts to see them;

I can't pick them up or love them—I do
Not know why. I can't take these
Dishes into me. They're strays, no one's.
I do not have a place to put them. My cup-
Boards are full and I hate my closed heart.
One night, late, the dad packs
The dishes into boxes, mixing up the settings
And I do not know where they are now.

Hurricane

Tonight the world is darker. I can't fly home.
Category Four. My mother calls my husband.
"This might be it." In her lawn, limbs.

Limbs I would recognize, she says. If
I came down. She has no water, no power.
At dinner Jacob says he met the Devil

Last night in his dreams. And the Devil
Was a great guy, a nice guy, not bad at
All. They shook hands. His normal hands.

Jacob's palms dance. See, like this. My mother's in
Her tiny closet, leaning into hung up pants. I say
Don't dream like that so much, Jacob. He peels

His apple. What, he says. What? In the window
Our family's reflected. We're missing some parts.
Where the light shines too brightly, heads lamps.

Weatherunderground.com shows the red cell
Pulsing over Lakeland, hounding Orlando.
My mom is a dot. On screen, this Wilma looks

Like something nourishing: juicy nut ringed with
Sweet furred skin gold and green. Where you
Are supposed to eat everything, even the hard white rind.

II.

I Don't Remember Telling the Stepsons

But when we drive down Gondola Drive,
My father's street in Orlando, while
I am trying to bend memory, shirts, yearning,
Stray conversations and these boys
Into something that looks like, to the
Untrained eye, anyway, a family
They say, This is where you jumped
Off the roof bleeding and This is the yard
Where you left your father for dead and
Here's where you sped with Todd Gele.
You made out with him over there.
We can't believe you spray painted
that guy's entire yellow Torino pink.

My new husband says, as we crawl
Down Orange Blossom Trail,
Why can't your schoolwork be this
Thorough, guys? And I keep saying,
This is all changed and I do not remember
Telling you any of these things.
(That's the Chi-chi's where you
Worked where everyone did cocaine.)
I do not recall remembering the car,
The kiss, the father left for dead, that
Motorcycle, my Orlando heart.

In those days I was thinking *Now*,
Not, *I'll marry a man with two boys—*
A three for one special—and raise them.
Then it was jackpot, fry chicken, syllables of
Ruin, it was possibly porn star baby
With shades of Actress, Saudi prince,
Dulcinea, Quiana, Candies and surf
Culture—I could see the sun rise on one
Beach and set over the other. This made
The world seem endless and me possible.
Did you ever get in trouble for anything?
The boys ask and the husband says,
Turn here? Tell me now or else.

When We Were Pinwheels, When We Were Daughters

The bronze mouth of the town, the outline of geckoes on my ceiling, the panties smell of my room, how oily my sweat used to be when I was a daughter. Get a grip! Don't be a fake! My legs were tan and strong. He bought me a motorcycle; *my father* loved to cook, he really got down with the food, steaks came *in the mail*. Every evening I enter memory's freaky caves, except when I don't. I see why we drink. Why we swim. Why we train to *break down*. If your father was a good bad man, then you remember, you have lived this way, always hungry, and you cannot bear him dead.

The Construction

In Michigan my house has been opened up.
I can't keep my hands and bones to myself.
I touched the blackened studs.
Water seeps down the insides of the walls.
I can't stop naming all the rooms.

I walked through with my father, houses
Under construction in Southern Oaks
Where we hiked up the temporary
Steps, my fingers in his belt loops.
This was before particle board when
Everything was unlocked,
When I didn't know: Death, psychosis,
Pornography and childhood
Make you so self-centered.

He pointed and I answered, hot water
Line, cold water line, breaker box.
This is where the water will pool,
Making life difficult for the family
Of four, the mice, the sofas, the cat,
The lamps and toys who will live here
Who will lock the doors, who will
Close the doors, who will live behind
Windows and hollow core and drywall.
Who will not ever know what the insides
Tasted like. What I know. What I put
There. What I wrote there.

From the houses going up my father took
Home copper pipe, what we called scrap:
Other men's tools, things. A thermos. We carried
Planks, circuit boxes, railing, stones, wire,
An arrowhead, a blue glass bottle, so much wire.

Everything important about a house is about water.
In leaves outside a house that would later burn,
He once stepped on a snake and didn't startle.

It was like they'd met many times before.

My house has a hole running through its center
And this dark water seeps, mold blooms. I want
To move. I want to build. But I can't. What he
Didn't explain: *you can get the girl*
out of the house but you can't get the house
out of the girl!

The Baby Dream Dreamed in Florida

This is the baby dream.
Before she is twenty-five
Years old every woman
In the world has it.

But you aren't the baby,
Don't think you are
The baby. Why do you
Think we have Jesus?
He Is The Baby.

Get in the backseat.
We are in the backseat.
(Before seatbelts, before God.)
Before your cheek is split
Open. Before your mother
Crying. Before your father
Pouring beer on her brown hair.
(Before he vacated the car,
The family, his male suit.)

Now: The engine idles.
You were never a doll girl.

A man's murdered that night.
At midnight, a man is always
Murdered somewhere.
In Your Dreams.
Baby. Look. How
They are taller, stronger

Than you. Look now
Those babies *run you down*.

Global Positioning

It's not hard to envision the demise of the paper road map,
In a generation or two, because a map, for all its charm
Is really a smorgasbord of chance information, most of it useless.
　　　　　　　—Nick Paumgarten, "Getting There," *The New Yorker,*
　　　　　　　April 24, 2006

Whenever I am asked, *How did you survive?* I lose my bearings.

I drew maps, named each street, compulsively lining reams of paper
　　with towns.
And then I drew floor plans for every house in town, placed each bed,
　　see insert A.

I mapped cities, a parallel life. I drew myself out. A map doesn't tell us
　　what we want
to know: *why this life?* A map is algorithm: if *this* is here, that's *that*;
　　there you go.

I placed a library in every quadrant, and train tracks and trees; every
　　street I drew I
Named; every line led *out of town*. Across the floor in the Florida room,
　　my lines continued

Off the paper, through my mother's house, that ocean crazed with inky
　　monsters,
Grimacing lacy denizens of the uncharted. Compulsion is always
　　an attempt to escape

The three basic geometric operations that orient all our experience:
　　Rotation, reflection
And sliding. Three illusions. I drew myself out. Don't ask how. Consult
　　your own

Demise, your map.

Lines from Manuals for Marriage

Attend weddings. As many as you can.

We've been walking down the aisle a long time.
Remembering all the boys we slept with.
You could call it insomnia. You could call it preparation.
One foot in front of the other, everyone watching.
We do it to ourselves.

In Today's Society, many females are marrying canines younger and younger.
There are some dogs tall as men.

Pay attention to the bride: stepping
Gracefully to the altar—a princess.
She's almost there—watch her.
The minister has sparky eyes, a black suitcase.
A ring the size of a collar.

Honeymoon dreams may have the consistency of a soup.
Do not be alarmed. It's normal.
Do not bore him with your dreams.

We know murdered girls. Before we are brides.
Blossom, Angie, Lisa. Amy, Rebecca, Chavonne, and Beth.
Not that anyone's counting.
Not that anyone is truly keeping track.

It's your guest list! Give it a special twist!
You have to use your flair.

She got the perfect flowers.
Their scent is throwing us off.
We planned it that way.

Before Children

His calls make me slippery, his phone lines
Spin shine. Cell phone rings and a million cells
Answer *Why not?* He's old enough to say
You're so young. I'm old enough to find this fun.

He can't give you a diamond, my friend explains.
Here comes the high hard one. Inside and tight.
I am sparking—an arrow. Not a bride.
Where is your control? she complains.

Lately I have not been losing my looks,
Just misplacing the key phrases associated
With beauty: spin, right now, curve red.
Baby fling that pill. I'll just marry books.

I Know What I Saw Last Summer

Mostly his back. We were on the motorcycle leaning
Into the speed limit dreaming of whole
Other nights, happiness, Florida, the unreconstructed
Shangrai-La Motel. Moon well-hung, low-slung.
I stuck my neck up around his, banging swan.
Our giant plastic heads clanking. Hanging on.
That moon: cold orange plastic ball foretelling *fall fall*.
I was pointing. But it was behind clouds, gone.

Fall. That was the first second of the end of it all.
So long, summer. Tonight I look up and see a slice
And remember there were two names for the moon
That month, names which no longer apply.

Listening to the New Tom Petty

I'm back in the sinkholes with the boy I loved
Most, left early. Florida bars in the scrub, raccoon shows

And oysters, frog legs, mullet, conch. Possum shacks on the river.
Seersucker. And his mouth: tan inside, salty, cold as a spoon.

I've heard he never married. I heard he drinks
Too much. I heard he whispers his own name. *Buzzards*.

He knew me when I knew me. I keep up.
I know all the words after one close listen. Everybody knows

The words to some songs in little bits and strands.
But I know these words as stray pieces too, even unsung.

I don't need a crowd, a verse, the bridge.
I don't miss him. I miss *her*. And how we laid on time.

Every Woman is Haunted by One Dress

In National City Bank on 8th Street, with my husband,
Applying for a home loan, the blue flowered
Dress I bought with a Parisian credit card in 1980
Pops back up, filmy rayon stalker. Youth's back in the form
of that size five blue and white dress, still killing
Me, crushing my credit rating: $49.99 in 1980, never
Paid, I do not know why. I loved the dress. It's five
Hundred dollars now, to clear things up. Thanks Loan
Officer Dave Hikkemma, three years happily serving
Customers like me. The interest, the penalties. My
Husband is shocked. We sign
For the loan, I write out the checks.
Signing my name, I remember way back when

Signing the slip, how I felt sick paying so much for a dress.
But it was white flowers on Dutch blue ground,
Princess seams, with a bow in the back, ballet length.
My first department store credit card. White sandals.
Afternoon on Lake Talquin, a pontoon boat, reading
A book. Dress in the trunk of my car, a secret, making me
Shudder.

Accredited, sick, at first I couldn't
Bring myself to wear the perfect dress.
For days it lay beating in its silky white
Crunchy bag, wrapped in sheets of tissue.
With its receipt, which I also have
Kept, like a birth certificate, pressed
Like a secret, like a hope, like a coupon
For becoming the kind of girl who wears
A beautiful summer dress and uses lotion
Regularly on the spots prone to roughness
And tearing. And cracking. Once I got started
Wearing the dress I wore it every day, as it is with
Pleasure. Until I faded from that dress. As it
Is with pleasure. I thought I'd given it away in
Tallahassee.

Yesterday, alone in my house, alone with my perfect
Credit rating, the home loan now long ago unloaned, I was

Sorting out what happened to me by way of going
Through stored clothes and closet things, a trusty old method.
And in a plastic tub with blankets and my mother's thinnest
Things, her nightgown, her beige gloves, her slips, a pink hat,
That dress, the blue-flowered paid-for dress, alive and well.
I couldn't believe how new it looked, how chatty. I sprang it
From the layers and it laughed; I put it on the Goodwill pile
On the top. When I'd had enough remembering, I drove that dress,
Some boring coats and mens' workshirts, and plastic cups
And baskets and vases and bad boots and Pendleton to drop-off.
But at the last minute, in the drive-thru I pulled out
The blue dress, it lay silky sly on my lap. Blooming, slender
And grinning like blackmail. I felt as though I had just about
Dumped off a kitten. And gotten caught.

This morning I washed it. I dried it in the sun. The dress
Is smaller than I remember, or things are bigger now.
And at noon today I stood in my kitchen, stripped and
Stepped in, worried as sin. Unsure it would
Fit, after all these years, like bad debt,
Wrong on me. I entered the dress, feet first.

Oh, I tucked right into the dress just fine: white
Flowers on blue rayon, E'spirit brand, that bow
Erect on the small of my back, those pockets
Sweet hopeful fill-me puffs on my thighs,
The mid-calf breeze and cap sleeves.
This dress is always a perfect dress.
No wonder it's everywhere I want to be.
Buttoned up and smoothed on me now
The dress says *of course it's a perfect fit.*
Silly, You haven't changed a bit.

Photograph of Debra and Heather at Glen Lake

We're arm in arm.
Our black summer
Sundresses touch at
Our shoulders, hips.
I love the sky
Between us
A girl part, a diamond
Of grey at waist.
A slit of not-us between us.
We are breathless.
As though we have swum
Across the plate
Of the lake without
Getting one drop wet.

We have received a
Letter from a reader and
A letter from a man:
They say there is too much sex
In the poems about our sons.
But in the photo
You only see we are friends.
You do not see mothers.
You do not see the boys
Between us. What we have
Written we have written
Because men are easily
Washed by women and
When they are too
Weak to say,
"No, do not
Leave me alone,"
We know there has to be
An explanation.

We are women. We forget
Men forget where
They came from, and how

Much love is cleaning up,
So much picking up after.
The lust piled in houses.
Wiped down, toweled off.
Folded and put back.
Remember desire
Originally meant
Here I have made a space
For you to be in
Sweet, here you are.

III.

Unstill Life with Stray Hair, Divorced Woman, and Tub

In my mid-life still life, there's only one skull. I
Am banging around in it. This disturbing meal I've made,
Eggplant gratin, cools on the counter. I get in the tub, shot
Of Chivas rimside, old Hazel Atlas glass, pearlized in the
Western sun. I like living in the house alone sometimes.

At first I thought it was a thin crack on my pristine porcelain.
Whose hair is this? Not mine, I'm all dark. Clear floss, black tail—
Which end is even up? Who has been in this house, what witch?
And why did a hair switch course, change its stripes, and when?
What thought did I have gone instantly from black to white?

Was it the afternoon in summer I realized my father may as well
Be dead the way he lives? Was it this past Tuesday, when I cried
Like a baby for a man to take the dead pigeon out of my garage
Where he lay on the shelf, behind poisons, his feathers, loose, puffed
Under his body like a terrible mattress? His protection his own deathbed.

I rise from the tub, dripping, steaming, not thinking Botticeli
As I usually do, because I am pinching the terrible single hair
Between my fingers. I have brushed death with more care
Than you, Hair, and I can change on you instantly too.
Held up to the light, this piece of hate mail from my skull, is mostly clear.

I press it out on my desk, between the phone book and a manuscript,
To measure. Dinner slumps deeper into the kitchen trash. By morning
The hair will be gone. But I do not know that now. Now I think
I have a chance. I still believe I'll find a ruler, save everything for closer
Study and understanding. Naked from my bath, still steaming, I'm hearing

The hair now, it's humming, clear violin string. The mature speech of objects,
Life: Keep seeing us this way. That's the arrangement.

Palm Sunday in Pew With Ex

I can't hold hands with him. Steal the song book.
I can sing in Spanish. Love his new shoes.
It's our anniversary—which we lose
When we divorce—a date. Kids with palms look

For those of us unpalmed; I hide my first,
Take three, four more. Minister, amped, selects
Death Where Is Thy Sting, a damp hymn my ex
Wholly knows: note, word, breath. I slit my wrist

Accidentally; blood beads. I knit, braid
What I divided, make a fan of what I frayed
While we sing. I have looked back inside
My old ring: today's date, I was a bride.

I forget it will always be ending,
Ends over again and again. And stings.

Kitchen Waltz with Kitty Wells, Moon, and Boys

The blinds are up, the dusty screens loose and you're working
On the dishes real slow and I am not helping. It's 9 PM, hot sticky
Michigan summer night, the lake out there, humming emptiness.
The boys play StarCraft online, hovered over the terminal
Stuck to cheap chairs, ones you brought home from Employee Sales.

It's September and still summer and still hot. We are still
In love in a kind of jagged way. I don't always love this life.
I'm still dreaming. You ask about my time. I go to the sink

Pull your hands from the dismal water, you into my arms. You
Are the better dancer from the waist up. I'm superior from the hips
To the floor. And then you put on the music. And the moon comes over
The steel sink. And the kids come in to see why. And you open
Another bottle of cheap Foxhorn chardonnay, which
We have convinced ourselves is golden good.

The boys don't dance they peck, chicken beaks. I dance no sex, family.
Just Fun Mom Dance Moves. I promise everything good for the boys
With my body, my smile, my barefeet. But they shrink, they back out.
They can't stand to see it, me and you, swinging, losing our rhythm.

The boys are back at their brilliant box, making finger explosions
In that weird blue light, and the dad and I move into our boxes
And balances. We took a ballroom class once. We know the words
To all of Wells. We know how to stage the moonlight, and move
Like any small dancing vague family.

Cookbooks in Bed with Ex-Husband on Side

My stomach is full of bok choy and garlic and greens
And I am reading *Local Flavors Cooking Essentials:
Everything you Need to Know About Cooking Anything
Perfect* and simple with impossible to find perfect foods
And I am happy, happy, happy. I do not want to make love.

I want to make risotto with lavender, chives, and sheep's
Milk cheese from a little mountain town outside Perugia.
I sleep with cookbooks. I have this thick hard pulsating one
On my low belly, where my desire is; I am sated and I am
Ravishing.

I can conjure persimmon stew with glory butter and muskmelon,
Crème fraiche with summer noodles. With you, I can't canoodle,
I've got four more new cookbooks, and I'm dreaming of dinners.
Oh, what is it about food on the sheets, the knife of your body
Sharp and silvery next to me. I'm full, I want to eat. I'm in love,
I want to prepare. I hear you sleeping. Maybe you are a little
Confused? Let me find fresh strawberries, let me make you my basic

Béarnaise. A little sleeping cap out of fruit and stem? Let me lick
You, or later; not by the book, not by the book, not by the book.

Acknowledgements

Prism: "I Don't Remember Telling the Stepsons"
Smartish Pace: "Language of the Couple"
Fugue: "Dating Men with Children"
Subtropics: "Listening to the New Tom Petty"
The Marlboro Review: "The Boys I Borrow"
The Blue Mesa Review: "When Does Life Begin" was titled "Wanted:
          Dead or Alive Baby"
Controlled Burn: "You Suck," and "Lines From Manuals for
     Marriage" under the title "We Do It To Ourselves"
The Seattle Review: "Grocery Store Parking Lot, Winter in Michigan,
     No Children" titled "Winter Grocery Store Parking Lot with
     War, Boys"
Confrontation: "When Does Life Begin?"
Natural Bridge: "Photograph of Debra and Heather at Glen Lake"
The Connecticut Review: "The Construction"

"Kitchen Waltz with Kitty Wells, Moon, and Boys" was published in
Sweeping Beauty: contemporary women poets do housework edited by
Pamela Gemin and Julie King, Iowa, 2005.

"When We Were Pinwheels, When We Were Daughters," and "We
Do It To Ourselves" appear in the *New Orleans Review* as part of a
series of seven collaborative collages with visual artist Jenny Krasner;
the full series of seven collage-poems is also part of an exhibition at
ThirdStone Gallery in Fennville, Michigan, curated by Bruce Cutean.
See www.thirdstoned.com and www.Jennykrasner.com

I am most grateful to Jackie Bartley, Bruce Cutean, Mark Halliday,
Jenny Krasner, Lorraine López, *Prism*, Debra Wierenga, and Katherine
Yanney. Thank you, Leslie and C.B. at Scusi's—you provide Poetry
Night a warm home. Priscilla Atkins and Greg Rappleye encouraged
these poems when they were young. Thank you to the boys for
sharing the controller. Deep gratitude to the late Herb Scott for
choosing this manuscript. And thank you, Elizabeth Marzoni and
Marianne Swierenga at New Issues.

photo by Face Photography

Heather Sellers is the author of two previous volumes of poetry, the short story collection *Georgia Under Water*, a children's book, and a series of books on the practice of writing. Her memoir-in-progress, *Face First*, describes life with prosopagnosia. Recipient of a National Endowments for the Arts Fellowship for fiction, Heather Sellers is a professor at Hope College in Holland, Michigan.
Her website is www.heathersellers.com.

New Issues Poetry

Vito Aiuto, *Self-Portrait as Jerry Quarry*
James Armstrong, *Monument in a Summer Hat*
Claire Bateman, *Clumsy, Leap*
Kevin Boyle, *A Home for Wayward Girls*
Jason Bredle, *Standing in Line for the Beast*
Michael Burkard, *Pennsylvania Collection Agency*
Christopher Bursk, *Ovid at Fifteen*
Anthony Butts, *Fifth Season, Little Low Heaven*
Kevin Cantwell, *Something Black in the Green Part of Your Eye*
Gladys Cardiff, *A Bare Unpainted Table*
Kevin Clark, *In the Evening of No Warning*
Cynie Cory, *American Girl*
Peter Covino, *Cut Off the Ears of Winter*
James D'Agostino, *Nude with Anything*
Jim Daniels, *Night with Drive-By Shooting Stars*
Joseph Featherstone, *Brace's Cove*
Lisa Fishman, *The Deep Heart's Core Is a Suitcase*
Noah Eli Gordon, *A Fiddle Pulled from the Throat of a Sparrow*
Robert Grunst, *The Smallest Bird in North America*
Paul Guest, *The Resurrection of the Body and the Ruin of the World*
Robert Haight, *Emergences and Spinner Falls*
Mark Halperin, *Time as Distance*
Myronn Hardy, *Approaching the Center*
Brian Henry, *Graft*
Edward Haworth Hoeppner, *Rain Through High Windows*
Cynthia Hogue, *Flux*
Joan Houlihan, *The Mending Worm*
Christine Hume, *Alaskaphrenia*
Josie Kearns, *New Numbers*
David Keplinger, *The Clearing; The Prayers of Others*
Maurice Kilwein Guevara, *Autobiography of So-and-So: Poems in Prose*
Ruth Ellen Kocher, *When the Moon Knows You're Wandering, One Girl Babylon*
Gerry LaFemina, *The Window Facing Winter*
Steve Langan, *Freezing*
Lance Larsen, *Erasable Walls*
David Dodd Lee, *Abrupt Rural, Downsides of Fish Culture*
M.L. Liebler, *The Moon a Box*
Alexander Long, *Vigil*
Deanne Lundin, *The Ginseng Hunter's Notebook*
Barbara Maloutas, *In a Combination of Practices*
Joy Manesiotis, *They Sing to Her Bones*
Sarah Mangold, *Household Mechanics*

Gail Martin, *The Hourglass Heart*
David Marlatt, *A Hog Slaughtering Woman*
Louise Mathias, *Lark Apprentice*
Gretchen Mattox, *Buddha Box, Goodnight Architecture*
Carrie McGath, *Small Murders*
Paula McLain, *Less of Her; Stumble, Gorgeous*
Lydia Melvin, *South of Here*
Sarah Messer, *Bandit Letters*
Wayne Miller, *Only the Senses Sleep*
Malena Mörling, *Ocean Avenue*
Julie Moulds, *The Woman with a Cubed Head*
Carsten René Nielsen, *The World Cut Out with Crooked Scissors*
Marsha de la O, *Black Hope*
C. Mikal Oness, *Water Becomes Bone*
Bradley Paul, *The Obvious*
Jennifer Perrine, *The Body Is No Machine*
Katie Peterson, *This One Tree*
Elizabeth Powell, *The Republic of Self*
Margaret Rabb, *Granite Dives*
Rebecca Reynolds, *Daughter of the Hangnail, The Bovine Two-Step*
Martha Rhodes, *Perfect Disappearance*
Beth Roberts, *Brief Moral History in Blue*
John Rybicki, *Traveling at High Speeds* (expanded second edition)
Mary Ann Samyn, *Inside the Yellow Dress, Purr*
Ever Saskya, *The Porch is a Journey Different From the House*
Mark Scott, *Tactile Values*
Hugh Seidman, *Somebody Stand Up and Sing*
Heather Sellers, *The Boys I Borrow*
Martha Serpas, *Côte Blanche*
Diane Seuss-Brakeman, *It Blows You Hollow*
Elaine Sexton, *Sleuth*
Marc Sheehan, *Greatest Hits*
Heidi Lynn Staples, *Guess Can Gallop*
Phillip Sterling, *Mutual Shores*
Angela Sorby, *Distance Learning*
Matthew Thorburn, *Subject to Change*
Russell Thorburn, *Approximate Desire*
Rodney Torreson, *A Breathable Light*
Lee Upton, *Undid in the Land of Undone*
Robert VanderMolen, *Breath*
Martin Walls, *Small Human Detail in Care of National Trust*
Patricia Jabbeh Wesley, *Before the Palm Could Bloom:
    Poems of Africa*